Shoving My Way Into the Conversation

Poems by Carl Nelson

ISBN:0692617906
ISBN-13:9780692617908

DEDICATION

For the greater good.

"To those progressive minds who labor to coerce our thoughts, our feelings
and our tastes for the greater good - to my mind the greater good is
determined by a fuller constituency and a longer span of time than your
notions realize."

- the author

Plays by Carl Nelson:
Into the Wild Blue Yonder
Personal Growth Through Copier Sales
Ollie's Day Out

Essays by Carl Nelson:
The Audience is a Mob

Poetry by Carl Nelson:
A Poet's Past Lives
Shoving My Way Into the Conversation

All are currently available through Amazon books.

CONTENTS

Acknowledgments   i

Dark Behemoth   1

The Majority Opinion   Pg 2

As Long as…   Pg 3

How to Get Your Poem Published   Pg 4

Ex-Patriot in Mexico   Pg 6

Ending Poverty   Pg 7

A School of Thought   Pg 8

Artis Amazonika   Pg 9

What You Pretend to Be is Part of Your   Pg 10
Relationship Too

All the While, It's Machines Enjoying Rising   Pg 11
Employment

The Vulgarity and the Horror of It   Pg 12

Nuts and Bolts   Pg 13

Sorry, It's Instinct   Pg 14

Submitting   Pg 15

Playwright's Lament   Pg 16

A Marriage Made in Heaven   Pg 17

Charles Bukowski   Pg 18

A Poetic Recapitulation, in part, of Robert   Pg 20
Murrays book, "By the People"

A Letter on Taste   Pg 21

Two Stanzas of Opinion   Pg 22

You're Gonna Be Like Me   Pg 23

Just Because You Imagine Something,   Pg 24
Doesn't Mean It Don't Exist

Friday Night Lights   Pg 25

Flag Waving   Pg 27

How Reality Feels   Pg 28

Poise   Pg 29

Global Warming   Pg 30

The Sound of Souls Released Prematurely   Pg 32

The Devil's Laughter   Pg 33

Wonk Veal   Pg 34

Herd Immunity   Pg 35

Jesus Casts Out Demons Into a Herd of Pigs   Pg 36

Most Likely, It Doesn't Matter   Pg 37

Poetry Makes Nothing Happen   Pg 38

Bloggers   Pg 39

Anarchist at the Political Fair   Pg 41

Big Government   Pg 42

By the Time...   Pg 43

ACKNOWLEDGMENTS

To my contrary nephew for my defining purpose:

"…creating an environment where reactionary thinking is tolerated."

Dark Behemoth

"In the beginning, the artist needs an audience to grow. Once mastery is achieved, the audience needs the artist's help to extend themselves."

In a portion of a play I wrote,
two salesmen grill a newbie
and are so consumed by their quibbling
they ignore his response.

The scene chewed its waters a few minutes -
like a great ship passing in the dark theater,
while I, the playwright, bellowed silently
in the quiet auditorium,
 "There is a behemoth passing through your fog, audience!"

In recompense I remember fondly
a scene from a play I directed,
where the characters became so alive,
they didn't need the audience -
breathing from the slow, glowing center of their concerns,
while crunching and gnawing the scenery
like two famished lovers.

You knuckleheads,
so puffed with your own lives,
take that!

The Majority Opinion

A progressive once held a referendum on gravity
so that we all could repeal or at least diminish it,
leaving us to skip about in a state of flippancy
where up and down had less basis in reality.
There was only centrifugal force and spin.

Having it mostly our way was like having it all
without the monetary investment.
Very popular! It lowered the overhead and reduced the payments,
rather like having a wealthy co-signer, sponsor
or patron.

Some held this person a sage or prescient,
for realizing the majority opinion,
by which all things are made certain,
was like winning, which is everything.

As Long as…

As long as people smoke,
exhale slowly and look up,
then fish for another in a crushed pack,
they will look for miracles.

As long as poets feel a phrase to write,
thinking deeply and free in a poem no one reads;
like a tree falling in the forest,
there will be questions about what exists.

As long as the prominent puff their cigars,
while tossing others dismissive looks,
disenchantment and alienation
will haunt cadres of the elected.

As long as people inhale, exhale, and stare across
in groups of two or more -
fifty feet from the entrance to any public building -
there will be head nods, sighs and quiet affirmations.

Cowboys sucking hand-rolled on board walkways,
private dicks lighting up femme' fatales in past celluloids,
private drive blue bloods with shined oxfords planted on their
running boards,
rebellious youth, loose women, and the unwashed, un-shaven, TV-
addicted,
and the innumerable unemployed sorry asses…
as long as people smoke, exhale and look up
there'll be something said - or left unsaid - to hang in the air.

How to Get Your Poem Published

Display obscure literary allusions and share idiosyncratic meanings
as if you had found them on the beach.
Turn them every which way as if they were bits of glass.
Don't make it too long unless it's unreadable.
Display a profound empathy for biodiversity.
Speak for those without a voice - but *not* for animals.
Remember, it's all about some unearthed trauma.

Don't tell, show sexual organs.
Display them.
These are our flowers!
Describe sexual penetrations repeatedly.
Also describe giving birth and suckling
in terms of leaking fluids.
Male readers should squirm.
Dwell on death and the inconsolable over and over,
over and over.
Detail how the unfathomable makes you *feel*.

Life will disappoint your poem. It will disappoint you.
It will disappoint your editor, your publisher and your reader...
if you are representing reality correctly.
Lie a lot, especially if it's the truth you reveal.
Use a cliché' people like -
not one they've grown used to.

Name drop, name drop, name drop...
Write very personal and embarrassing things
in a way that people can pretty well guess who you mean.
A good way would be to dedicate the poem to someone famous - but
contemporary.
It's no good if it's plain you could never have known them,
and this could not be an authentic personal revelation.

Asphalt roads are bad.
You are ambivalent about gravel.
Dirt roads are better, but a dirt path is best
which diminishes then vanishes into wildness
is what you are going for.

Ex-patriot in Mexico

I know how they appeared:
lovely as brown Aphrodites
stepping from their shells
to lounge, wiggling their toes in your frontal lobes
to the gentle slap of surf
and the gurgle of pina colada
through the pale, lime-colored straw.

In Mexico, all things are possible,
even plausible.
But you never understood the language,
the terms were never settled,
and she's going back into the sea.

Time to move along there, Gringo.

Ending Poverty

He raised his voice to ask,
"You want the rest of that?"
before I'd even begun to eat.
In fact, while still walking.

But stopped. Big mistake!
To look at him.
He was dirty, filthy in fact.
Looked as though he'd peed himself.

Was wrapped in a soiled and stained wool overcoat.
But it was his portly insoucance
with one eyelid turned inside out
that whispered of comedy -
that "sweet and sour dramedy"
we all respond to.

It began innocently enough
when I gave this fellow half my sandwich.
It was a pretty good one -
a toasted hot pastrami and ham, melted havarti
and a couple slices of vine ripened tomato garnished with basil.

A School of Thought

There are words
which slide you along
like an icy sidewalk,
'curling' you towards the goal,
to slip on the meaning
and hit hard,
maybe bruise a few parts in the process,
in a faux pas' ballet,
wherein what happens is the shock.

Those poets who lack enduring love,
and yet sell the frisson;
must lead lives of some difficulty.

Artis Amazonika

"I think the reason we have so much trouble coming together as a nation is this cult of individualism we worship."
-*Female Workshop Instructor*

(Coming together would certainly be more manageable,
if no individuals existed…
way before the problem escalated,
or tumesced, for sure.)

She has *pleasant* mastered.
Granted, one of the nicer Heras I've ever encountered,
a languid pre-modern with fanciful gestures.
To contradict her would be like strangling a kitten.
They'd come after me with spears.

I remember the Amazons and fear
why those Grecian limbs are missing.
And I imagine sticking mine out,
getting my priapus up and shellacked as thus…
or lopped off, and then lost to the ages,
as a vanished sexual aid of former times.

To resurface inevitably as another dated relic
from the green, slimy, hoary keep of male glories;
cleaned up and restored beside the turkey basters,
in a crystalline case with an informative plaque
on a white plaster pedestal
in a gallery of wealthy white matrons
meeting and milling
on the correct side of history.

What You Pretend to Be Is a Part of Your Relationship Too

Basically, you're gonna be what the market will respond to.
There's no other way to explain it.
It's operant conditioning. It's relentless. It's what people expect, literally.
They pay you attention, so you've got to give them what they've paid for.
It's as simple as that.
What does it matter to them, who you are?
Because they have *needs*. You get it?
That's why it is important to make who you pretend to be
an important part of your relationship, too.
It's the money-maker. It's the crowd-pleaser.
And it's the part of you which you really have some control over.
You might think of it that way, as a matter of fact.

Who controls who you *really* are? *God*, right?
Well, there you go. Pretense is your only chance at free will, my friend.
So grab the gold ring. Go for the musto. Get into the game.
"You are who you pretend to be." And now you know why.

All the While, It's the Machines Enjoying Rising Employment

Q: "Why did the unemployed cross the road?"

A: "To get to the other side and fashion themselves romantics."

The answer being education - and the problem being graduation:
the *un, under, partly-employed* and *over* qualified,
with insulated mugs and laptops,
stuff coffee, tea, and Viet Pho shops ,
their heads buzzed to distraction.

These well-read proliferate
 wherever their computers whirrrrr...
Our future's on these
who pass the time typing lustily,
living in-between and on the down lo
in runs behind firewalls.

These burgeoning articulate, who hold court without offices
pulling favors from the air
breathing across a 2% lo fat el Grande,
while vying with poets for the chairs.

The Vulgarity and Horror of It

The facts of life are very conservative, it is said.
But civilization itself is a libertine
forever chastising her young
to be decent and embrace charity -
to cultivate the weed alongside the vegetable,
to raise the wolf with the lamb.
And as the libertine prods this processional -
one meek voice boasting to cheer louder for its mommy than another
-
to proliferate and inherit in the upwelling hysteria,
eventually the wolf - being more wolf-like -
is the more merited,
preferred and protected both in law and opinion,
until sated.

Nuts and Bolts

If only atheists could believe in nothing,
they would be no more trouble say,
than a lamp or a table.
 Or, at least, I wish the percentage of citizens
who regularly worship State Entities
and Social Justice were decreasing.

The underdog is just another *dog*, people.
For God's sake, look around.
Just like the poor -
the richer will always be with you.

If we are hoping to hold this Republic together...
Hell, if you are hoping to hold *anything* together -
a marriage, a car, or a dishwasher -
you must have bolts as well as nuts.

It does no good to struggle with connection,
for which you already have a thousand nuts,
and order a thousand more.
You must at least entertain the *idea* of a bolt!

It all reminds me of a play I once critiqued.
"It needs a Republican," I said.
"You can't get where you're going
 with the cast you've created," I emphasized.
They stared at me as if I were the moon.

How much longer can they stare at people,
as if they were the moon?
Way beyond the pale,
and incomprehensible.

Sorry, It's Instinct

It was a great awakening
to realize my thoughts did not make me
of interest to others.
It was a bright day outside,
and I found it hard to believe -
as if one of the Basic Rights of Man
had been violated.
But there it was:
that I could breathe and yet be cultural debris,
trash set on the corner curb for pick-up.
It was as if the small village where I had been raised
had been burnt to the ground, or par broiled.
It was as it there were cracks in the great egg, earth;
my keepsakes scorched, ruined and broken.
My accepted faith had expelled me, and there it was:
that most of life was the pursuit of audience,
and so degenerates into theater as Shakespeare described it.

Now, even the years teach me
that celebrity and leadership are also a State of Grace.
"Many seek, but few are chosen."
We are born of a substance with questionable beginnings,
leading a confused existence towards uncertain ends.
Clarity has been a hall of mirrors.
And the culture has flowed like a terrible flood
seeking the lowest level, and carrying all before it.
Raw power prowls in the silt and hollows like catfish.
Raw power - there's the current and perennial thing
to waggle its tail in the shallows,
whiskers snuffling in the mud,
and rise as the next King.

Submitting

"Submit: to yield, give in, cave in, back down, capitulate…"
- Websters

"Do you have any letter,
(a word, or phrase even),
of introduction?"
"Who do you know? Where have you published?"
You may drop any name you have
heavily in this space _____.
(We have all had to begin somewhere.)
They want to know if you can even follow direction.

"What are your qualifications for writing a poem?"
(Is your soul on fire?)
"What are your credentials?"
(Take them out and push them under the glass, please.)

"Why aren't we soliciting you?"
(Is God working mysteriously again?) (smiley face)
 "Realize we get more than (5,390,324,852,610)
…*enough* submissions per month,
of which yours is just…
one."

…

"We would like to reject you *personally*,
but time simply does not *allow*.
So please do not be offended by this form response.
Your interest is of vital importance to us."

"Enclosed is a subscription form.
Respectfully, the Editors."

Playwright's Lament

Every artist has a theory for why their success plateaus.
I subscribe to the Big Bang Theory.
First there's this Big Bang!
And then my audience is moving away from me
at incredible speeds
on all fronts
even distancing themselves from one another
in a sort of pandemic of repulsion -
to soap themselves liberally.

Not to stigmatize my efforts,
but there's a case to be made that I *might* have alienated
or perhaps, at least, ruined for some people
a small sector of this fragile frisson'
which is live theater.
Atomizing the collective.
Destroying, or at least, undermining
what there once was of a common bond.
Rending its fabric -
which, I'll admit,
I should have washed on *delicate* -
until I am some "lone voice crying in the wilderness",
musing "across the surface of the deep".
Crying out into the emptiness.

A Marriage Made in Heaven

The Attending said, "listen to the patient, they will tell you what is
wrong."
Sometimes that would be listening a very long time, to a very long
list…
until you had to say, "Okay, enough. We need to focus."

There's the mind you're speaking with,
and the body you're looking at.
And they have a relationship you're guessing at;
kind of like a marriage.

And like getting into an discussion
between a man and his wife,
it can be calamitous
to be caught in the vicinity and sharing intimacies…
There's portions of the relationship
for which the mind feels ashamed.
Like a compulsion, you must understand.

They haven't any idea how they got here,
or came to be, with no control over it.
And their bodies must have felt for their minds,
as any dumb brute would, which… has feelings,
but must bellow for respect.

Charles Bukowski

With his enormous egotism, he wrote a roomful of sentences
across wine stained papers on a scratched and stained aluminum
kitchen table,
where the alcohol was poured from a plastic Kool Aid pitcher,
his flaccid haunches pressed to the ripped seat
of a plastic upholstered aluminum-tubed chair
till they ached to move.

Here's a man reliving his miserable youth as a balls-out affair,
always dusting off the used and re-used for another try.
Something picked up off the street and dusted off, like his
Imagination,
to perch up on a barstool and pour a few drinks into
until she pinked up, began cussing, choking, showing a little life,
then shambling off to the head to vomit.
Offering nothing nutritious. I wouldn't pick the guy for a do-gooder.
Bukowski, bellowing his blousy machismo, was a scrupulous poet
of life's darkly comic brutality.
He'd sit and chat her up a bit.
And maybe later, if it came to that, and neither had passed out -
they'd have sex. Some kind of sex.
Not out of any special affinity. For Godsakes! nothing sentimental.
But as another way to pass the time, would be the proper way to do
it...
Being of opposite sexes and seemingly the natural next step...
A man needs *something* to write about. Just drinking's not enough.

I've seen books by Bukowski in libraries and urinals,
Motel 6's, Big 'O' tire stations... pharmacies.
And even pee soaked, they bequeath to their feckless surroundings a
style -
or plucked from the bookcases in mansions,
pressed in between those hard-bound and glossy
dust covered biographies of power.

"Don't try," is his graveside quotation,
outside of where the monuments pose.
He was the plastic colored snack sack blown by the wind,
pasted to the busted cemetery parking lot cyclone fence;
the warm, half-drunk beer
left on a soiled tin-trimmed counter.

A Poetic Recapitulation, in part, of Robert Murrays book, "By the People"

As the framers designed it,
government was to be limited.
But progressives wanted to accomplish things,
and saw the Federal Government
as their best possible organ.

This all began in the late 19th century,
but really blossomed in 1937
with the Supreme Court's ruling in
Helvering v. Davis,
which destroyed the Federal Government's
limits on spending.

Then, with the Supreme Court's capper ruling
in *Wickard v. Filburn*
the Federal Government was allowed to regulate
all areas of business.

It all revolved around whether the Government
was authorized to "provide for…
the general welfare".
And once the progressives had it decided
that the Federal Government *was* there
to provide for the general welfare -
boy, did they get started.

This led to the present plethora of governmental activism
which has embedded it into
each and every of the furthest reaches
of the citizens' lives
in a Kafkaesque scenario
fit for Cable TV.

A Letter on Taste

The current intelligentsia worship correct taste,
which I hate.
Not my own, of course.
But I try to keep it penned
and disciplined
like a large, demonstrative dog.

Not so with these others.
They love their purebred
and let it roam freely.
They let it sniff me intimately
as if I were strange
and feared animals
in general and am not...
an intelligent person.

Of course, I object vociferously,
and point out that they need to keep
their entitled mongrel of the upper castes at bay
and more disciplined and cognizant
of proper behavior.
Before *my* dog rips *theirs* a new one.

Which to them,
only proves a point,
that I am a *hater.*
The sort of person an enlightened community,
in its effort to evolve into a more perfect *village*
and raise more perfect children
will eventually have to deal with...

as they all know
dogs understand and see things
ordinary souls can't.
And this is about where we are now.

More later

Two Stanzas of Opinion

People back here seem quick to take offence,
and are suspicious of being reasonable,
as if you were a waffler or deceptive.
Are you 'fer me or 'agin me, their blank looks seem to say.
'Well, I'm 'fer you, but that could change at any moment',
seems to be an answer they respect.

They do not like you implying you know something they don't.
But toss it out there offhand like a bit of foolishness;
grease it with enough of that and they'll listen...
with suspicion.
Then paint the demon with their own colors,
thank you very much.

My son said the other day upon exiting Home Depot,
he thought the people in the store are
"afraid of you".
Granted I'm six foot eight, three hundred pounds,
with wildly mused hair, flaring eyebrows and speak softly,
almost jokingly, my odd ideas and conceptions.
But it's my threat, which seems to be coming across well.

You're Gonna Be Like Me

"Go ahead, do what you want.
But you're gonna end up like me."
That's what I tell 'the Kid'.
"There's no two ways around it,
you're around me too much.
Even when you can't help yourself,
you're imprinting,
like a little baby chick!"

"And do you know
when I know
that I've been effective?
When you start criticizing me for the same things I criticize you. Ha!
Music to my ears! That means you're *internalizing*."

"Sure, you might turn out to be rich or famous.
But that would just be a rich or famous aspect of *me*.
Or you might become a criminal,
but you'd still be *my* kinda guy
'cause I've raised you through your *formative years*."

You know what I see when people complain about their kids?
It's people who don't know themselves so well.
So, "you know what it is when I complain about *you*?
It's because you're *taking too damn long!*"
I shake my finger.

...to get to be me.
When everything will be fine.

Just Because You Imagine Something, Doesn't Mean It Don't Exist

Most things that exist
(maybe *everything?*)
were first imagined.
And this includes *you.*

Just look around yourself
and there is a good chance
most of what you see was first imagined.
Most of it is young
as you
and was still being imagined -
the initial agreements and bills being shoved
under bar napkins -
before you appeared.

They say God is *imagined.*
First appearing to Adam or Eve,
every bit as solid as a serpent or a tree.
Then the both of you having a very forthright conversation.
Remember?
Which, of course, you went right out and violated.

Nowadays, however, He seems to be slipping away
into some Faraday-like equation.
The proposal, agreement and drawings left to idle on the shelf,
while others claim all of the solidity
and have grabbed all the toys.

That's the thing about having kids.
"How sharper than a serpent's tooth it is to have a thankless child,"
said Shakespeare
and is a sentiment
as yet to be improved upon.

Friday Night Lights

The people in my favorite TV series
grab my thoughts
more than the people around me.
I worry about them more than my family.
It's as if the national franchises have taken over
running my personal relationships out of business.
And "Friday Night Lights" is the current WalMart.

I can't get enough of poor coach Taylor's struggles,
or pissed enough at that disloyal Bobby -
as I was almost getting to like him.
And those poor teens struggle so…
I told my own to "Shut up!"
if he didn't want to watch.

Tami Taylor, the coach's wife,
is not only the essence of class and beautiful,
but is more understanding
and has the best advice…
always hitting the right note,
always pressing the correct button.

Tyra Collette's beauty stands like a colossus
astride Gibraltar
and outlet to the Mediterranean.

And Matt Saracen works so hard and is so loyal
he could make my dog jealous,
and maybe fret a bit
about his own position at the food bowl.

And Tim Riggins is boyish steel.
Doesn't say much.
Is tough as they come.
Loves football, beer, girls…
and *always* makes the big play.

Honestly,
I can't think of anyone in my life
who compares.

Flag Waving

I love how the flag's stripes twist and fold
in the warm breeze moving up the Ohio,
through the Appalachians
on a quiet street in the late afternoon.

That bright presence
up and down the street slowly lifting,
clean as cotton, sleek as rayon,
curling in a funnel shrinking,
then unrolling, unwrapping, the rustle and the flapping,
the popping and the slapping,
waving from porches up and down the street:

the reds of flags against the green of trees.

How Reality Feels

Wild charity. Wild justice. Wild love.
Most of the time you can't get near it.
It's like one of those covert ops on TV, who says,
"I'll be in touch."

When a great calamity hits
and people are asking?
"How could God allow this?"
My first thought is,
'Maybe we don't understand God very well.'

And when an atrocity occurs
and people ask,
"How could a loving God allow this?"
My first thought is,
'Maybe we don't understand love very well.'

And when people began discussing
"the reality of the situation"
I wonder, 'Where are we getting all this?
Off the internet?'

Poise

About the moral high ground,
God told them what He thought:
that Job and his friends hadn't a gnat's conception of things.

But as to poise…
It must have seemed to God a thing
so unforeseen and unusual
as to have charmed God, Himself,
that He had made it.

Until then, God had re-tooled His image,
monotonously reproducing selfies until…
His image ran off!
took it above and beyond,
balanced upon that thin thread
above the abyss and below the heavens.

And in that long moment Job was allotted,
while dangling over that existential dread,
God had made of man a pretender,
a diabolical capable of balance on a whim,
with a sang froid
and a faith so admirable
the Lord Himself must have gasped
at His creation.
This something - in the face of the existential, to be studied
in the dark absence of His nothingness -
was a breakout Achievement
and Conception even God could play with.

Global Warning

First it was Global Warming, and the Seas Were Going to Rise and Drown Us.
The seas didn't rise. The Maldives are still there.
And Global Warming is now Climate Change.
Then a Great Shelf of Ice was supposed to dislodge from a Melting Antarctica,
 fall into the water, and… the Seas Were Going to Rise and Drown Us.

A little back story: After fears in the 1970s of Global Cooling had abated,
Y2K was going to destroy civilization in the year 2000,
and then Second Hand Smoke was going to kill us.
But from there on out, the playbill got a lot more crowded,
as various performers realized something a lot of us fully allow
both In and Out of Government, and On Both Sides of the Question.
And that is that "A Crisis is a Terrible Thing to Waste".

So next up, and coming soon! are melting methane beds, from deep within a dying ocean…
expect a cold vortex pushing south, down from Canada, in between
summertime projections of starving, drought-stricken farmers
moving up from the south,
a flood of undocumented aliens carrying ebola,
(insert where appropriate: the dissolution of our shorelines and possibly Manhattan)
 ISIS fanatics running rampant across all of the mid-East, and thence
to disseminate by air to everywhere where they might find you, and
an atomically armed Iran.

Exacerbating the crumbling financial picture from within the
European Union,
either Greece, Italy, Spain, or all three could default. Or Germany -
that economic engine - could pull out altogether leaving the whole
European Consortium to collapse like a circus tent.
The High Pressure Fracking for oil in the Fly-over States, which
could possibly destroy all potable water,
is also challenging the dominance of the former oil-rich countries,
who came about their oil too easily,
putting their regimes in jeopardy creating more and more instability,
in a soon to be nuclear armed Near East.
While the newly created, well-paying blue collar jobs and cheaper oil
in the heartland
 is fuelling the rush to more fracking, even cheaper oil, and ever more
CO_2,
plus a lot more money-enhanced Bubbas , exacerbating the chances,
Climate Change Will Occur, as it always has in the past, or that we
will Be in Denial all the while we have our air conditioners turned up
high.
So maybe yes, at least, to that.

"97 out of 100 scientists believe excess CO_2 causes Global Warming."
This is what we are told, even by the President.
What was actually determined was that,
"97 out of 100 scientists believe excess CO_2 *contributes* to Global
Warming."

So, say the Doubters, "Just me being *alive* contributes to Global
Warming, as does my friend's pug dog's farts."
"And the President *contributes* to Global Warming every time he
speaks!"
And probably much more so than me. Nevertheless,
by the President's measure, I'd guess we could say that he personally
has caused Global Warming.
And that 97 out of 100 scientists (plus me!) would agree on this.
Fair enough.

The Sound of Souls Released Prematurely

"The Kingdom of God is within you and around you," Jesus said,
perhaps predicting by 2,000 years
the advent of the Civic Symphony.
The earth's sounds are various,
whereas music is imagined and makes evident our soul.
Music could be the sound of souls released prematurely
and let out for a a pre-flight check of the ears,
like Johnny Appleseed planting his nurturing seeds
to apple a New Jerusalem.

You say, "See all these people walking around with ear buds?
I don't think they are experiencing the Kingdom of God."
Perhaps not, but they are souls surely tempted.
Old Beelzebub raps soundly on the door of Beethoven's Ninth.
Pop souls hear glistening Apples crunching, Bathsheba's charms,
Satan's power.
They tour Sodom and Gomorrah,
or marvel at that showroom Baal 4x4 with all terrain tires,
bouncing up and down on its Baal shocks,
cantering up those mean streets to hip hop accompaniment.
And the Firebird could well be an angel shimmering.
Nothing's changed much.

Though the Devil is in constant improvisation,
while the Lord's path is straight and true
with quarter notes predominate.

The Devil's Laughter

The story of Adam and Eve gets it right.
We hide how God made us.
It's the central story of who I am,
and I would guess of who you are,
reborn, cursed actually, to take that same bite daily.

Just as the surgeon cuts the skin
to reveal the other world within
running us like CIA operatives.
So I am as I appear to you
but not to me, really.

Staying alive - socially, economically, and otherwise -
like Jews in the Shoah -
there is much to be ashamed of!
There are not enough fig leaves in the Garden
to cover all of this compound interest on our Original Sin.

I suppose this is why the Devil is so bitter.
As soul truth teller, he can't suppress his smirking
at a God who has fastened all of his love and longings
on this ridiculous toy,
too ashamed of its Being
to even look at Itself,
walking about in the world He's given,
with a face palm, eyes shut tight, and head shaking.
It's like Christmas morning, turned to the Crucifixion, then Easter.
And the Devil is shaking (with laughter).
It's too funny, really.

Wonk Veal

Birthed in hate-free environments,
raised on milk with cold cereal condiments
until late into their twenties,
in messy bedrooms fixated on computers,
in an ever expanding digital universe where the pull of reality -
like the restrictions of gravity - is a slight percentage of ours,
these pale, flabby, neotenic, metro sexual specimens of careful
procreative planning
hormonally infused in a environment
as sterilized for moral hazard and ethical quandary as hydroponic
tomatoes
cook up well when you're a politico spinning a crisis.
They join together like legos in a transformative manner
to battle micro-aggressions and real oppression.

Here is a Brave New World of Atheists - who run on Belief;
reduced and reconstituted in a simmering post-modern incubator;
laboratory tested, authenticated, systematized and thoroughly vetted
by university empanelled, blue-ribbon commissions.
One hundred percent guaranteed (with a codicil of "zero tolerance")
to hate greed, racism, sexism, all forms of inequality,
social injustice, environmental degradation, and to embrace all forms
of love,
including locally grown vegetarian festivals,
with added moral and ethical supplements plus artificial preservatives
such as student aid and interest free loans added for extended
adolescence,
in an environment of continual learning,
much like Mao's permanent revolution
where personal expression and the aha! moment have replaced due
diligence.

Herd Immunity

Opinions kept buttery biscuit warm and fresh as pups stacked and
snoozing,
touching each other in the soft reassurance of correctness as far as
touch can go…
It's a kind of ego-inflation, or rather, ego-multiplication, I'd suppose.
Becoming more than themselves, much more… *many* more… to be
precise.
We are the world! or, at least, the largest part of it.
That's the idea..
Egalitarian in emphasis, they love to move collectively
to sniff the butts and howl!
Yelling, running, attacking whatever threatens;
their biggest difficulty being the need to pee.

You'll find a pretty strong rim of stench around most packs,
causing the other forest creatures to grumble,
"My God, how can they live like that?"
"A look inside their warren, and it's a mess,
with not a dog there
that takes personal responsibility!"
"One must possess some interlocking jigsaw piece of mentality;
to pass the crazy/dog test.."
Touching each other in the soft reassurance of themselves as far as
touch can go,
it's a kind of ego-inflation, or rather, ego-multiplication, I'd suppose.

Jesus Casts Out Demons Into a Herd of Pigs

Love something and otherwise reasonable people
will react as if you'd popped the question.
Admire beauty and they'll tell you why.
To be arrogant is human, I suppose;
to be humble, sublime.

Think of any great calamity or any great sin
and the reasons in retrospect
would seem quite frail and thin.
Really shocked, I mean *embarrassed*
to be seen as they were.

Spin, that whirlwind of reason…
the Patron Saint of Confusion,
the original Tower of Babel;
reason gone to the fair and stuffed with cotton candy and giddy rides,
always entreating us to view the problem from another perspective,
from the next amusement,
never wants to stop and talk or to reflect.

But, "by their fruits you will know them."
Is there a better perspective than that?
"Consider the lilies of the field…" Jesus still entreats
such *reasonable* people as aren't so sure this world even exists,
and others carried away by ideas of alternate realities,
and the perceptual impossibilities of any certain truths.

"Oh, shut up!" I confess
I could lose it also
and send all that advanced cognition flying
into a herd of pigs
to spur the demons' oinking and squealing.

Most Likely, It Doesn't Matter

"We are governed, our minds are molded, our tastes formed, our ideas suggested, largely by men we have never heard of." - Edward Bernays in "Propaganda"

I'd thought I had opinions,
but on reflection
what I'd thought were opinions
were mostly reactions, fulminations.
Like when someone pokes you with a stick
or prods you on the head with a sharp rock -
that is, posits a provocation -
and you think, "Sh*t!", or get fed up.

Blind reactions are the modern coin of the realm,
generated like bitcoins by admen, terrorists, political operatives,
all stripes of schemers and the media in full view.
A zealot can be delivered with certitude
a reasonable man cannot.
My irrational reaction is political currency,
a sort of gold standard redeemable most anywhere
and at all times.

In court, a piece of evidence can be ruled inadmissible
and so prejudicial as to be excluded.
In the media however,
"if it bleeds, it leads".
So less of import is reported more and more,
I'd guess, because it doesn't matter.

Poetry Makes Nothing Happen

"The world is full of magical things patiently waiting for our senses to grow sharper." - Yeats

In the thoughtful magazines currently,
poetry is given the corner here and there
to be displayed like the family crest
proving descent from nobility.

Poems are not invited to the full event
but left in the antechamber
with the other unwashed petitioners
and fed in the scullery.

Because poetry is about everything , everybody, all of it.
With all the riff and the raff,
its take on life is so broad
  "Poetry makes nothing happen."
Nevertheless…

It is very hard to make nothing happen.
Zen Buddhists can only get one hand clapping.
Full Buddhists work their lives at it.
And it took the Lord seven days.

Bloggers

A lot of bloggers live like prophets,
who push their way through stale cups of coffee, or cans of flat
Pepsis,
onto the blogosphere, now and then,
to warn about something or other which is at odds
with either Natural Law or God's Plan.
Like the Old Testament prophets who awoke one day,
and hurried off to tell someone… preferably the King.

Prophets who start shouting long before the city's entrance,
waving their arms and role playing as they tread the weary miles,
so that it's the best and most current recapitulation
of God's will as can be divined.
Prophets who aren't going to trust it to an epistle
submitted conventionally to fall behind a desk
in a 12 by 10 anonymous tan manila envelope
certain to have followed the accepted format, with NO multiple
submissions,
submitted after reading up a bit on the King's expected audience,
that is, where his appeal lay,
so that what God had in mind might fit well within the King's
agenda,
at least during the reading season,
all the while recalling, that it wouldn't have hurt to have subscribed,
to the herald's Daily Pronouncement,
or note that you were a longtime, loyal listener
before commencing to speak.

Nope. These guys made it fresh as newly squeezed orange juice
served up with full pulp before the King.
Lord, it must have been glorious.
They just strode in and grasped that Kingdom by the ear.
God's will be heard!
Or fear the wrath.
That's the way this shit happened way back before the slush pile.
All this insight coming in over the transom.
The King was beside himself. Each day a new message.
God was setting them straight regularly, and roughly!
Imagine (being as the King, way up there) listening…
all the while wondering…
if the sand were going to swallow you up,
and burp out the crown?

Anarchist at the Political Fair

If we are our own worst enemy
as we so often are,
what folly to cast aspersions!
I am not here to rile you up;
I am here to calm you down...
Continue to disagree as you will and as you must.
I am not here to change your minds - but to disperse them!
Altogether we constitute a pox! There's the truth of it.
Too much power is granted to too few.

The government prints more money to stay financially able,
and the Congress passes more laws to finance more campaigns.
Be quiet. Think first. Request nothing and refuse what they offer.
No one needs participation in a debacle!
Disperse as friends. Just walk away
and history will record this day a success.

CARL NELSON

Big Government

Sometimes I lie in bed at night
trying to imagine how big the government is
until I pass out.

And summer times I some times,
lie on the grass
and name each constellation
as a separate bureau.

That constellation there.
The big one.
That's the Department of Health, Education and Welfare
with a total budget this fiscal year 2015
of one trillion twenty billion dollars.

Each season new bureaus populate the skies.
All these nebulae of governmental bodies,
moving away from us at light speed
in a grand expansion!

…entities upon entities
beyond
the furthest reaches of visible light.

By the time...

By the time it comes to violence and the lines are drawn,
it's bigger than a warm casserole,
beyond a smile and an open hand,
and about the size of heroics.

By the time they're executing some and torturing others
with clips, prods and electrodes,
it's beyond reasonable debate and collegial discord,
and nearer the nature of an imminent threat.

By the time our neighbors are rounded up and placed in pens
to be shipped away on trains to be gassed,
it has moved beyond respect for competing opinions and free
expression
and headed beyond a crisis.

Which was a terrible thing to waste,
by the time they've sown hatred, chopped off limbs, raped and killed,
sowed disorder and spread famine;
by the time they've got you by the balls
and your heart and mind are pledged to follow.

ABOUT THE AUTHOR

Carl Nelson spent twenty years in the Seattle theater community, during which time he wrote and produced plays, directed others, and performed whenever the talent was missing but a body still needed. Before that he did stand-up comedy.

The author lives in Belpre, Ohio where he moseys about. Writing poetry makes him happy.

www.ingramcontent.com/pod-product-compliance
Lightning Source LLC
Chambersburg PA
CBHW060541030426
42337CB00021B/4375